YOUR KNOWLEDGE HAS VALUE

Bibliographic information published by the German National Library:

The German National Library lists this publication in the National Bibliography; detailed bibliographic data are available on the Internet at http://dnb.dnb.de .

Imprint:

Copyright © 2016 GRIN Verlag
Print and binding: Books on Demand GmbH, Norderstedt Germany
ISBN: 9783668657410

This book at GRIN:

https://www.grin.com/document/415929

Samira Penner

Happiness economics. How to measure growth and welfare?

GRIN Verlag

GRIN - Your knowledge has value

Since its foundation in 1998, GRIN has specialized in publishing academic texts by students, college teachers and other academics as e-book and printed book. The website www.grin.com is an ideal platform for presenting term papers, final papers, scientific essays, dissertations and specialist books.

Visit us on the internet:

http://www.grin.com/

http://www.facebook.com/grincom

http://www.twitter.com/grin_com

FOM Hochschule für Oekonomie & Management

Studienzentrum Düsseldorf

Assignment

im Modul

Economics

über das Thema

Happiness economics: How to measure growth and welfare?

Autorin: Samira Penner

Abgabedatum: 2016-12-10

Table of Contents

List of Abbreviations

Cf.	compare
DUP	Düsseldorf University Press
Eds.	editors
f.	and the following page
ff.	and the following pages
GDP	gross domestic product
HDI	Human Development Index
MDP	Measure of Domestic Progress
MEW	Measure of Economic Welfare
p.	page
SDSN	Sustainable Development Solutions Network
SWB	subjective well-being
UNDP	United Nations Development Programme
Vol.	volume
WVS	World Value Survey

List of Symbols

α   Alpha

β   Beta

ε   Epsilon

List of Formulas

$$W_{it} = \alpha + \beta X_{it} + \varepsilon_{it}. \tag{1}$$

1. Introduction

Regarding the topic of this assignment, this first introductory chapter will provide the situational context through the problem description, present the central objectives and outline the general scope of work of the assignment.

1.1 Problem Description

Everybody wants to be happy. There is probably no other goal in life that commands such a high degree of consensus, because to most people, happiness is all they want and try to achieve. Thus, happiness has long been considered the ultimate human goal in life. Even Aristotle considered happiness the ultimate motive for all human action. In today's consumer culture, this happiness is often pursued in the marketplace. Yet, economists have refused to deal with individuals' happiness a long time but considered it to be an "unscientific" concept.[1]

However, in the past few years the situation has changed and economic science has experienced the introduction or reintroduction of individuals' happiness into economics. While traditionally economics has almost exclusively focused on consumption, wealth and other monetary indicators to measure individuals' well-being, it now more and more adopts the subjective notion of well-being to analyze how economic determinants such as income, wealth and employment as well as non-economic determinants such as personality traits and socio-demographic factors affect individuals' utility and life satisfaction. Although Easterlin already examined correlations between economic growth and welfare and individual happiness, it still took about twenty years for the idea to take off. In the meantime, happiness research and economics has provided many interesting findings and insights. Today, there is a wide range of

---

[1] Cf. Frey, B. S., Stutzer, A., Testing Theories of Happiness, 2005, p.116-146; Frey, B. S., Stutzer, A., What Can Economists Learn from Happiness Research?, 2002, p.402ff.; Frey, B., Stutzer, A., Happiness and Economics, 2002, p.vii; Ahuvia, A. C., Friedman, D. C., Income, Consumption, and Subjective Well-Being, 1998, p.153; Dixon, H. D., Controversy, 1997, p.1812.

literature on the so-called happiness economics that analyses individuals' well-being and its determinants.[2]

1.2 Objectives

The objective of this assignment is to find out if economic growth and welfare affect happiness and if yes, to what extent major economic indicators such as income, employment and inflation are able to measure and contribute to individuals' level of happiness.

Thus, the assignment establishes the link between economics and happiness and does not present just another theoretical work on the mere theoretical base but provides empirical results from the current state of happiness research as well as a critical review of the measurement results and outlines the limitations of the mentioned economic determinants regarding their scope and validity.

1.3 Scope of Work

In order to provide the mentioned transfer from the theoretical base to the empirical findings and their critical review, the assignment follows a specific methodological and deductive approach. The logical line of thoughts implicates the formal structure of the assignment, which in detail is composed of the following four main chapters:

Chapter 1 "Introduction" is essentially a formal chapter which serves as a guideline to present the basic concept of the assignment through the problem description, objectives and scope of work.

Chapter 2 "Theoretical Approach: Economics of Happiness" presents the theoretical foundation of the assignment by outlining the economic context of growth and welfare. In addition, this chapter bridges the gap and establishes the connection between economics and happiness by outlining the concept of happiness economics

---

[2] Cf. Jahan, S., Human Development Report, 2015, p.iv, 24; Haucap, J., Heimeshoff, U., The Happiness of Economists, 2014, p.2; Lis, J., Nutzen oder Glück, 2014, p.11-14; Frey, B. S., Stutzer, A., Recent Developments in the Economics of Happiness, 2013, p.ix; Selin, H., Davey, G., Happiness Across Cultures, 2012, p.1; Peil, J., van Staveren, I., Handbook of Economics and Ethics, 2009, p.202; Clark, A. E., Frijters, P., Shields, M. A., Relative Income, Happiness, and Utility, 2008, p.95; Frey, B. S., Stutzer, A., Testing Theories of Happiness, 2005, p.116-146; Van Praag, B., Baarsma, B., Using happiness surveys to value intangibles, 2005, p.225; Dixon, H. D., Controversy, 1997, p.1812f.

through a broader definition of happiness and its elusive concept as well as the scope of current happiness research and measurement.

Chapter 3 "Practical Analysis: Relevance of Economic Performance on Happiness" provides the transfer of the theoretical approach into practice through analyzing the influence of the major economic determinants income, employment and inflation on happiness by presenting the empirical results from the current state of happiness research. Moreover, this chapter provides a critical review of the measurement results by outlining the limitations regarding their scope and validity.

Eventually, the assignment is completed by chapter 4 "Closing", which again is a formal chapter to respond to the initial problem statement and objectives of the introductory chapter 1 by providing a summary and conclusion of the essential findings of the assignment as well as a future outlook on the developments in the area of happiness economics.

This composition is based on a wide range of internationally recognized standard works and references as well as latest discussions found in high-quality economic journals and online papers that provide information on the current state of happiness research and measurement.

2. Theoretical Approach: Economics of Happiness

In the context of the presented situational setting, the following chapter will present the theoretical base to the concepts of economic growth and welfare, their traditional measurement and the new development of happiness research and measurement in economics.

2.1 Economic Growth and Welfare

The term economy derives from the Greek word oikonomos, which means "someone who manages a household". In fact, households and economies have much in common. A household faces many decisions and must allocate its limited resources among its various members, just like a society. The study of how society manages and allocates these limited resources through a system of markets is called economics. Once a society has allocated its resources, it must also allocate the output of goods and services produced. "The percentage increase in the number of goods and services produced in an economy over a period of time, usually expressed over a quarter and annually"[3] is known as economic growth.[4]

In this context, welfare economics is defined as "the study of how the allocation of resources affects economic well-being"[5]. There are two main distinctions of economic well-being, subjective and objective well-being. While objective well-being refers to measures of the quality of life and uses economic determinants and measures, SWB (subjective well-being) is defined as "the way in which people evaluate their own happiness"[6] that can be determined by both economic and non-economic factors.[7]

Economic well-being of a society is often measured by the GDP (gross domestic product) which is defined as "the market value of all goods and services produced

---

[3] Mankiw, G., Taylor, M., Economics, 2014, p.9.
[4] Cf. Mankiw, G., Taylor, M., Grundzüge der Volkswirtschaftslehre, 2016, p.1-2; Wessels, W. J., Economics, 2012, p.2; Heilbroner, R. L., Milberg, W., The Making of Economic Society, 2011, p.47; Samuelson, P. A., Nordhaus, W. D., Economics, 2010, p.4.
[5] Mankiw, G., Taylor, M., Economics, 2014, p.169.
[6] Mankiw, G., Taylor, M., Economics, 2014, p.169.
[7] Cf. Mankiw, G., Taylor, M., Economics, 2014, p.169.

within a country in a given period of time"[8]. In fact, the GDP measures two things at once: on the one hand, the economy's total income and on the other hand, the total expenditure on the economy's output of goods and services.[9]

Thus, the GDP per person presents individuals' average income and expenditure in the economy and therefore seems a natural measure of economic well-being. However, the GDP does not consider the distribution of an economy's income but the GDP per person only gives information on the situation of the average individual although there is a wide range of individual situations and circumstances behind. In addition, the GDP only considers paid work as a monetary value while unpaid work such as household and care work remain largely unmeasured although they lead to the production of goods and services as well, e.g. food for own consumption, collection of water and firewood, housecleaning, laundry and care of children.[10]

Thus, the validity of the GDP as the ultimate measure of well-being has become a controversial issue. Sure, it measures the ability to obtain the necessary input factors for a worthwhile life and thus a large GDP may present an indicator for a high standard of living of a society but not necessarily for individuals' happiness. In addition, there are other economic as well as non-economic determinants contributing to individuals' quality of life and SWB that the GDP and other economic measures do not consider.[11]

2.2 Happiness Economics

Despite the significant increase of the GDP in many industrialized countries over the last 50 years, multiple studies prove that regardless of the increase in income and access to material goods and services the perception of individuals' happiness has not really changed that much. Increased wealth has not brought a similar increase in

---

[8] Mankiw, G., Taylor, M., Economics, 2014, p.439.
[9] Cf. Mankiw, G., Taylor, M., Grundzüge der Volkswirtschaftslehre, 2016, p.628; Jahan, S., Human Development Report, 2015, p.13, 206, 249; Frey, B. S., Stutzer, A., Recent Developments in the Economics of Happiness, 2013, p.xii; Heilbroner, R. L., Milberg, W., The Making of Economic Society, 2011, p.89; Samuelson, P. A., Nordhaus, W. D., Economics, 2010, p.650.
[10] Cf. eds. Helliwell, J., Layard, R., Sachs, J., World Happiness Report, 2016, p.4, 7; Mankiw, G., Taylor, M., Grundzüge der Volkswirtschaftslehre, 2016, p.643-645; Jahan, S., Human Development Report, 2015, p.117, 249; Frey, B., Stutzer, A., Happiness and Economics, 2002, p.36f.
[11] Cf. eds. Helliwell, J., Layard, R., Sachs, J., World Happiness Report, 2016, p.4; Mankiw, G., Taylor, M., Grundzüge der Volkswirtschaftslehre, 2016, p.643; Dixon, H. D., Controversy, 1997, p.1814.

happiness but surveys have shown relatively stable rates of happiness in those coun-tries. A group of economists have studied this apparent paradox and stated that "on average, people are no happier than they were fifty years ago"[12] in relation to West-ern societies.[13]

In 2006, someone called Cliff Arnall had developed a formula for calculating and quantifying the state of happiness. Although the scientific basis of this formula was disputed, it provided the necessary trigger for a discussion and debate on what is understood by the term happiness and the effects of individuals' way of life on SWB.[14]

2.2.1 Definition and Concept of Happiness

Any discussion of the theory first requires a definition of the term. What is happiness? This simple question is probably one of the oldest in the history of mankind and prob-ably also as difficult to answer.[15]

The greatest human minds have struggeled with this issue and many efforts have been made in defining what a happy life is and which circumstances make people happy. Ruut Veenhoven for example defines happiness as "the degree to which an individual judges the overall quality of his life favorably"[16], in other words meaning how well an individual likes his or her life. However, there has not been any clear understanding and consensus of what happiness is. There is a wide variety of differ-ent concepts involved in the everyday use of this term. It means different things to different people and is open for everyone to define for themselves what happiness is.[17]

---

[12] Mankiw, G., Taylor, M., Economics, 2014, p.450.
[13] Cf. Mankiw, G., Taylor, M., Grundzüge der Volkswirtschaftslehre, 2016, p.644; Clark, A. E., Frijters, P., Shields, M. A., Relative Income, Happiness, and Utility, 2008, p.95f.; Easterlin, R. A., Income and happiness, 2001, p.465; Frey, B. S., Stutzer, A., Happiness, Economy and Institutions, 2000, p.919f.
[14] Cf. Mankiw, G., Taylor, M., Grundzüge der Volkswirtschaftslehre, 2016, p.644.
[15] Cf. Frey, B., Stutzer, A., Happiness and Economics, 2002, p.3; Veenhoven, R., Is happiness relative?, 1991, p.2.
[16] Veenhoven, R., Is happiness relative?, 1991, p.2.
[17] Cf. Lis, J., Nutzen oder Glück, 2014, p.14-19; Peil, J., van Staveren, I., Handbook of Economics and Ethics, 2009, p.204f.; Frey, B., Stutzer, A., Happiness and Economics, 2002, p.3.

Because happiness is such an elusive concept, the terms happiness, well-being, SWB, satisfaction and welfare are employed interchangeably throughout this assignment.[18]

As mentioned before, there are generally two opposite concepts of happiness: subjective happiness and objective happiness. At one extreme, there is subjective happiness that refers to individual's life satisfaction from the internal perspective and at the other extreme, there is the concept of objective happiness which comes close to the idea of utility for identifying the extent of happiness from the external.[19]

Individual well-being is not an isolated feeling but strongly depends on the conditions in which the persons concerned live. Thus, social comparisons are of great importance and have to be taken into account. In addition, individuals do not have a fixed once and for all grid for measurement but they adjust to changing circumstances.[20]

2.2.2 Happiness Research and Measurement

Happiness research and measurement has been one of the new developments in economics in recent years and has already provided a substantial amount of new insights and findings. Current research is guided by the question about which factors affect individuals' happiness and how, supposing that measuring the state of happiness requires a set of determining criteria. In this context, economists and psychologists have found a strong correlation between individuals's perception of their own happiness and certain factors that are contributing such as socializing, relaxing, praying, meditating, eating, watching TV and shopping as well as health and the level of education and income. Other influencing factors refer to the question whether individuals are single, married or divorced, working, unemployed or retired.[21]

---

[18] Cf. eds. Helliwell, J., Layard, R., Sachs, J., World Happiness Report, 2016, p.12; Jahan, S., Human Development Report, 2015, p.71; Easterlin, R. A., Income and happiness, 2001, p.465.
[19] Cf. eds. Helliwell, J., Layard, R., Sachs, J., World Happiness Report, 2016, p.11; Frey, B., Stutzer, A., Happiness and Economics, 2002, p.4-6.
[20] Cf. Frey, B., Stutzer, A., Happiness and Economics, 2002, p.6.
[21] Cf. Mankiw, G., Taylor, M., Grundzüge der Volkswirtschaftslehre, 2016, p.644; Frey, B. S., Stutzer, A., Testing Theories of Happiness, 2005, p.116-146.

Out of these criteria it is possible to formulate equations for deriving a measure of happiness. These have been tested by both economists and psychologists and proven to be surprisingly reliable from a statistical point of view. One of the leading thinkers in the area of happiness economics is Professor Andrew Oswald from the University of Warwick in Great Britain who developed the following formula:[22]

$$W_{it} = \alpha + \beta X_{it} + \varepsilon_{it}$$

In the context of this formula, W_{it} denotes the self-reported level of happiness or SWB of an individual i at a specific date or period of time t and X a set of determinants assuming that they affect this well-being at a specific period of time. These could be economic determinants, such as income, but also demographic, such as gender, for example. The final term in the formula represents an error term, which serves to capture the possible influence of other unobserved factors on the final outcome. Thus, an individual's happiness has a cognitive aspect and is affected unexpectedly strong by his personal aspirations and expectations in life referring to the extent that they have been met.[23]

Knowing something about the factors that contribute to individuals' happiness allows for developing a measure that is better at reflecting this well-being than the GDP does, because monitoring and assessing human well-being in a changed world has to go beyond what was developed years ago and demands for exploring new and alternative measures and tools. One such measure is called the MDP (Measure of Domestic Progress) which counts on many of the factors connected to economic growth but also takes into consideration the relative effects and other factors that the GDP calculation leaves unconsidered. There are further suggestions for more effec-

[22] Cf. Mankiw, G., Taylor, M., Grundzüge der Volkswirtschaftslehre, 2016, p.644; Frey, B., Stutzer, A., Happiness and Economics, 2002, p.30f.; Dixon, H. D., Controversy, 1997, p.1813.
[23] Cf. Mankiw, G., Taylor, M., Grundzüge der Volkswirtschaftslehre, 2016, p.644; Frey, B., Stutzer, A., Happiness and Economics, 2002, p.30f.

tive measures of well-being such as the MEW (Measure of Economic Welfare) developed by James Tobin and William Nordhaus in 1972 as an extension of the GDP, the Index of Sustainable Economic Welfare devised by Herman E. Daly and John B. Cobb in 1989 which in addition takes into account income distribution as well as the deriving Genuine Progress Indicator. Another concept is the HDI (Human Development Index) developed by the Pakistani economist Mahbub ul Haq and published by the UNDP (United Nations Development Programme) in 1990 as a measure that assesses human well-being from a broad perspective, going beyond income.[24]

However, none of these new alternative concepts have yet succeeded to find acceptance as a universal measure of well-being. The attempt to measure subjective human behavior and expose it to rigorous science still represents a challenge to economists. Having some form of happiness index would be a good thing but yet there seems to be no ultimate measure that is perfectly complete.[25]

---

[24] Cf. eds. Helliwell, J., Layard, R., Sachs, J., World Happiness Report, 2016, p.5, 29; Mankiw, G., Taylor, M., Grundzüge der Volkswirtschaftslehre, 2016, p.644; Jahan, S., Human Development Report, 2015, p.1, 3, 71f.; Frey, B., Stutzer, A., Happiness and Economics, 2002, p.38.
[25] Cf. Mankiw, G., Taylor, M., Grundzüge der Volkswirtschaftslehre, 2016, p.644.

3. Practical Analysis: Relevance of Economic Performance on Happiness

Identifying the determinants of happiness it is useful to distinguish between five different types:[26]

- Personality factors
- Socio-demographic factors
- Economic factors
- Contextual and situational factors
- Institutional factors

In recent years, economists have contributed significant research on the effect of economic factors on SWB. The following chapter will critically survey and interpret the results of past research from an economic point of view.[27]

3.1 Economic Determinants on Happiness

There are three economic determinants which have an influence on individuals' happiness and SWB:[28]

- Income
- Employment
- Inflation

The following chapters will give emphasis on these variables which indeed turn out to be crucial as they have been proved to be the mayor economic determinants on happiness for the reason that happiness is dependent on material factors and eco-

---

[26] Cf. Lis, J., Nutzen oder Glück, 2014, p.20-23; Frey, B., Stutzer, A., Happiness and Economics, 2002, p.10f.; Frey, B. S., Stutzer, A., Happiness, Economy and Institutions, 2000, p.919f.

[27] Cf. Frey, B., Stutzer, A., Happiness and Economics, 2002, p.10f.

[28] Cf. Frey, B. S., Stutzer, A., Testing Theories of Happiness, 2005, p.116-146; Frey, B., Stutzer, A., Happiness and Economics, 2002, p.71.

nomic prospects. Thus, it is impossible to account for differences in happiness between individuals without without taking into account income, employment and inflation.[29]

3.1.1 Income

The thesis that a higher income leads to a higher level of happiness seems only logical at first, because a higher income expands countries' and individuals' opportunities in terms of access to more goods and services that can be consumed. Thus, it seems obvious that these two go together but in fact, higher income does not always lead to more satisfaction. The main reason for this paradox is that there are other circumstances changing with the higher income and after a certain period of adaptation, individuals' SWB is not significantly higher than it was before the increase.[30]

Only some economists have recognized this paradox, among them one of the first to seriously study the data on the reported level of happiness, Richard Easterlin, who concluded that "money does not buy happiness"[31]. Another one called Tibor Scitovsky even argued that a high level of income implicates continuous comforts and thus prevents the pleasure that results from incomplete and discontinuous satisfaction of desires.[32]

In order to discuss the relationship between income and happiness, three different aspects have to be taken into consideration in terms of comparison. First, a comparisons between countries as a whole to find out if individuals in rich countries are necessarily happier than those in poor countries. Second, a comparison over time to

---

[29] Cf. Frey, B., Stutzer, A., Happiness and Economics, 2002, p.10f., 71.
[30] Cf. eds. Helliwell, J., Layard, R., Sachs, J., World Happiness Report, 2016, p.12, 58; Lis, J., Nutzen oder Glück, 2014, p.25; Peil, J., van Staveren, I., Handbook of Economics and Ethics, 2009, p.202f.; Van Praag, B., Baarsma, B., Using happiness surveys to value intangibles, 2005, p.224-246; Stutzer, A., The role of income aspirations in individual happiness, 2004, p.89f.; Frey, B. S., Stutzer, A., Testing Theories of Happiness, 2005, p.116-146; Frey, B., Stutzer, A., Happiness and Economics, 2002, p.73; Easterlin, R. A., Income and happiness, 2001, p.465.
[31] Frey, B., Stutzer, A., Happiness and Economics, 2002, p.74.
[32] Cf. Lis, J., Nutzen oder Glück, 2014, p.10f; Frey, B., Stutzer, A., Happiness and Economics, 2002, p.73f.; Dixon, H. D., Controversy, 1997, p.1813. Oswald, A. J., Happiness and economic performance, 1997, p.1817; Veenhoven, R., Is happiness relative?, 1991, p.1.

prove whether an increase in income raises the level of happiness and third, a comparisons between individuals to conclude whether people with high income are happier than those with low income.[33]

Regarding the comparison of happiness between countries, various studies provide convincing evidence that individuals in rich countries are on average happier than those living in poor countries. This result has been established in an extensive study covering a large number of countries measuring data on happiness from the WVS (World Value Survey) which is the best source for international comparisons of life satisfaction. Another examination of several cross-national studies also concluded "a strong indication ... that personal satisfaction rises with the level of economic development of the nation"[34]. The effect of higher income on happiness is however identified as a curvilinear relationship, meaning a higher income provides happiness at low levels of development but once a certain threshold has been passed, a further increase in income has only little or even no further effect on happiness.[35]

In addition, a higher income has a positive effect on other indicators that again have an influence on happiness. Thus, a sole comparison of happiness between countries is only of limited value as the positive correlation between income and happiness may be produced by other factors and conditions going with income.[36]

Comparing the relationship of income and happiness over time on the example of the United States, scholars have identified that there has been a high increase of income over the last decades. However, this high increase of material well-being was accompanied by a modest decrease in average happiness and the proportion of people considering themselves to be very happy over the same period. This result

[33] Cf. Frey, B., Stutzer, A., Happiness and Economics, 2002, p.71.
[34] Frey, B., Stutzer, A., Happiness and Economics, 2002, p.75.
[35] Cf. eds. Helliwell, J., Layard, R., Sachs, J., World Happiness Report, 2016, p.4, 11f., 24; Jahan, S., Human Development Report, 2015, p.iii; Lis, J., Nutzen oder Glück, 2014, p.26f.; Clark, A. E., Frijters, P., Shields, M. A., Relative Income, Happiness, and Utility, 2008, p.96; Stevenson, B., Wolfers, J., Economic Growth and Subjective Well-Being, 2008, p.4, 8-25; Peil, J., van Staveren, I., Handbook of Economics and Ethics, 2009, p.203f.; Frey, B., Stutzer, A., Happiness and Economics, 2002, p.75f.; Frey, B. S., Stutzer, A., What Can Economists Learn from Happiness Research?, 2002, p.416ff.; Lucas, R. E., Clark, A. E., Georgellis, Y., Diener, E., Unemployment, 2002, p.9f.; Ahuvia, A. C., Friedman, D. C., Income, Consumption, and Subjective Well-Being, 1998, p.155, 159ff.; Oswald, A. J., Happiness and economic performance, 1997, p.1829.
[36] Cf. Frey, B., Stutzer, A., Happiness and Economics, 2002, p.75f.; Dixon, H. D., Controversy, 1997, p.1813.

is contradictory to the findings presented previously that people in richer countries are generally happier. There are of course many possibilities to explain this odd finding but it can also be an indication that "money does not buy happiness"[37] or that there are more determinants to SWB than just income.[38]

In this context, it is important to take into account the process of people adjusting to past experiences and changing circumstances. Happiness is somehow relative, because individuals rarely make absolute judgments but rather tend to draw comparisons from their environment, the past or expectations of the future. Over the life cycle, this causes deviations in aspiration levels. Thus, an increase in income initially provides a higher degree of happiness but after some months, people become acclimated to this new standard on which they measure their achievements, meaning their aspiration adjusts upward to the higher income and the level of happiness is not much higher than it was before. Additional material goods and services only provide extra happiness temporarily and don't bear lasting effects on individuals' well-being. The level of happiness depends on change and decreases with continued consumption. This process is called adaptation and makes people strive for ever higher aspirations, just as Samuel Johnson stated in 1776 that "life is a progress from want to want, not from enjoyment to enjoyment"[39]. Thus, individuals' happiness is determined by the gap between aspiration and achievement.[40]

Comparing people with different incomes living in the same country at a specific point in time to assess the effects of income on happiness, it seems at first that people

---

[37] Frey, B., Stutzer, A., Happiness and Economics, 2002, p.77.

[38] Cf. eds. Helliwell, J., Layard, R., Sachs, J., World Happiness Report, 2016, p.4; Frey, B. S., Stutzer, A., What Can Economists Learn from Happiness Research?, 2002, p.413-416; Peil, J., van Staveren, I., Handbook of Economics and Ethics, 2009, p.203; Frey, B., Stutzer, A., Happiness and Economics, 2002, p.76f.; Dixon, H. D., Controversy, 1997, p.1813; Oswald, A. J., Happiness and economic performance, 1997, p.1818.

[39] Easterlin, R. A., Income and happiness, 2001, p.465.

[40] Cf. eds. Helliwell, J., Layard, R., Sachs, J., World Happiness Report, 2016, p.12; Lis, J., Nutzen oder Glück, 2014, p.49-53; Frey, B. S., Stutzer, A., Recent Developments in the Economics of Happiness, 2013, p .xiiif.; Peil, J., van Staveren, I., Handbook of Economics and Ethics, 2009, p.202f.; Clark, A. E., Frijters, P., Shields, M. A., Relative Income, Happiness, and Utility, 2008, p.99-106; Stutzer, A., The role of income aspirations in individual happiness, 2004, p.90f., 95-103; Frey, B. S., Stutzer, A., Testing Theories of Happiness, 2005, p.116-146; Frey, B., Stutzer, A., Happiness and Economics, 2002, p.6, 77-81; Easterlin, R. A., Income and happiness, 2001, p.465; Diener, E., Suh, E. M., Lucas, R. E., Smith, H. L., Subjective Well-Being, 1999, p.277, 285f.; Ahuvia, A. C., Friedman, D. C., Income, Consumption, and Subjective Well-Being, 1998, p.156ff.; Oswald, A. J., Happiness and economic performance, 1997, p.1829; Veenhoven, R., Is happiness relative?, 1991, p.1, 3-6.

with higher income have more opportunities to achieve goods and services they desire as well as a higher status in society. However, research in happiness has proven that income does not buy happiness but in fact, "people are really seeking non-material goals such as personal fulfillment or the meaning of life and are disappointed when material things fail to provide them"[41]. In this context, happiness seems priceless as it cannot be achieved by material factors.[42]

The comparison of income and happiness at a specific point in time in a specific country has been the subject of a large empirical literature. The general results indicates that happiness and income are indeed positively related but differences in happiness among individuals can only be explained very little by differences in income. In fact, there are other important factors to explain why some people are happier than others, in particular economic determinants like employment and inflation but also non-economic factors like health. A number of other non-economic factors such as age, gender and education also have a positive effect on happiness, but a smaller one.[43]

3.1.2 Employment

The analysis of the relationship between employment and happiness generally considers two contrasting assumptions. On the one hand, unemployment can be considered involuntary and as an unfortunate state to be in due to a relatively short-term disequilibrium phenomenon. On the other hand, unemployment can also be voluntary in the sense that individuals choose to be unemployed because they find the burden of work and the wage paid unattractive compared to being unemployed and getting unemployment benefits and leisure. As a choice of alternatives, it would therefore only seem logical that the second situation does not affect individuals' happiness in contrast to the first.[44]

---

[41] Frey, B., Stutzer, A., Happiness and Economics, 2002, p.81.

[42] Cf. Frey, B. S., Stutzer, A., What Can Economists Learn from Happiness Research?, 2002, p.409-412; Frey, B., Stutzer, A., Happiness and Economics, 2002, p.81.

[43] Cf. Frey, B. S., Stutzer, A., What Can Economists Learn from Happiness Research?, 2002, p.409-412; Frey, B., Stutzer, A., Happiness and Economics, 2002, p.81ff.

[44] Cf. Frey, B. S., Stutzer, A., Testing Theories of Happiness, 2005, p.116-146; Frey, B., Stutzer, A., Happiness and Economics, 2002, p.95, 107f.

- 15 -

However, the effects of personal unemployment on happiness have been analyzed in several studies using happiness data, which contrast strongly with the latter assumption that unemployment is voluntary and does not affect happiness. In fact, all of the empirical studies find that unemployed individuals are much less happy than employed ones with otherwise similar characteristics. According to these findings, unemployment has a substantial negative effect on the SWB of the individuals experiencing it. This decrease in happiness is not necessarily or solely a result of the reduction in income but even in the case of compensation through social security the unemployed still suffer major psychological and social distress, such as isolation, loneliness, anxiety and depression or the weakening of their position in life and society. The insights gained from research open up the view of work, shifting from only being any activity that leads to the production and consumption of goods and services in terms of economic value to a central activity in life that contributes to a broader human well-being. On the job, people feel skillful and challenged, supporting the view that having work increases happiness while not having work causes unhappiness. However, it is not merely having a job but also other aspects as different types of work and occupations as well as experienced work satisfaction that matter in terms of human happiness and therefore need to be considered as well.[45]

3.1.3 Inflation

Inflation is defined as an increase in the general price level and often measured by the consumer price index. When dealing with the role of inflation on individuals' happiness, it depends a lot on what kind of inflation takes place, meaning the distinction between predicted and unpredicted inflation. When the price increase is predicted, individuals have the possibility to adjust to it. By contrast, when the price increase is

---

[45] Cf. eds. Helliwell, J., Layard, R., Sachs, J., World Happiness Report, 2016, p.12, 58; Jahan, S., Human Development Report, 2015, p.30, 35f., 98; Lis, J., Nutzen oder Glück, 2014, p.34f.; Frey, B. S., Stutzer, A., Recent Developments in the Economics of Happiness, 2013, p.xivf.; Helliwell, J., Huang, H., Well-Being and Trust in the Workplace, 2011, p.747-767; Cornelißen, T., The interaction of Job Satisfaction, Job Search, and Job Changes, 2009, p.367-384; Frey, B. S., Stutzer, A., What Can Economists Learn from Happiness Research?, 2002, p.419ff.; Frey, B., Stutzer, A., Happiness and Economics, 2002, p.96-100, 107f.; Lucas, R. E., Clark, A. E., Georgellis, Y., Diener, E., Unemployment, 2002, p.5; Di Tella, R., MacCulloch, R. J., Oswald, A. J., Preferences over Inflation and Unemployment, 2001, p.335-341; Frey, B. S., Stutzer, A., Happiness, Economy and Institutions, 2000, p.919f.; Ahuvia, A. C., Friedman, D. C., Income, Consumption, and Subjective Well-Being, 1998, p.155, 163; Oswald, A. J., Happiness and economic performance, 1997, p.1823f.

unpredicted or even comes as a shock, such adjustment is not possible. According to this assumption, the commonly held opinion of academic economists is that only unpredicted inflation reduces happiness while a constant but low and predictable inflation is not thought to cause any major problems as contracts and wages can be fully adjusted by the individuals to the expected price increase.[46]

However, combined time series cross-section happiness studies have analyzed the development of inflation in several countries over the course of time and came up with different results. The notion held in theoretical economics does not correspond to the insights gained from happiness research but the respective studies suggest that inflation has a substantial effect on individuals' happiness and SWB quite irrespective of whether it is predicted or not. Either way, it causes a reduction of happiness as individuals dislike inflation and particularly fear a decrease in their purchasing power and thus also their standard of living.[47]

3.2 Critical Review

The task of measuring individual's happiness and SWB is a difficult one and the paradox findings suggest that the presented results of happiness research cannot be accepted uncritically for different reasons.[48]

First, only careful analysis of multiple studies can determine if and to what extent economic factors influence individual's level of happiness. However, such analysis is barely possible as there is only little research available so far and thus a lack of strong evidence.[49]

Second, it might be argued that the responses to happiness questions are not reliable. The principle way in which happiness has been measured within the scope of studies available is by undertaking surveys. Although considering combined cross-

---

[46] Cf. Jahan, S., Human Development Report, 2015, p.206; Frey, B., Stutzer, A., Happiness and Economics, 2002, p.111-115.

[47] Cf. Frey, B. S., Stutzer, A., What Can Economists Learn from Happiness Research?, 2002, p.422; Frey, B., Stutzer, A., Happiness and Economics, 2002, p.111-115; Di Tella, R., MacCulloch, R. J., Oswald, A. J., Preferences over Inflation and Unemployment, 2001, p.335-341; Frey, B. S., Stutzer, A., Happiness, Economy and Institutions, 2000, p.919f.

[48] Cf. Oswald, A. J., Happiness and economic performance, 1997, p.1830.

[49] Cf. Ahuvia, A. C., Friedman, D. C., Income, Consumption, and Subjective Well-Being, 1998, p.155, 158, 161.

section studies, there are still measurement issues regarding the reliability and validity of the respondent's replies, depending on their honesty about their feelings as well as possible biases resulting from the context in which the surveys are undertaken.[50]

Third, there is the problem of comparability of such measures. As already mentioned, happiness is an elusive concept and left free to be defined individually. Thus, the ambiguity about happiness itself makes it very difficult for comparing as there is no common understanding of the term.[51]

Nevertheless, the presented findings of these kinds of studies are so far the only ones available. Despite the mentioned limitations and shortcomings, the general conclusion is that the measurements, though not perfect, do reflect individual's level of happiness to a reasonable extent which allows for determining major influencing factors on SWB.[52]

The main problem as with every challenging research question is the reduction of complexity to set up general assumptions. Thus, although each individual is free to define happiness in his or her own terms, in practice there are some dominant influencing factors on happiness that are pretty much the same for most people. Instead of trying to compare the happiness of individuals directly to one another, the approach is to break down individual notions to a comparable level – not only concerning the understanding of happiness itself as well as the set of influencing factors but also the underlying natural processes of adaptation and unpredictably changing aspiration levels.[53]

---

[50] Cf. Easterlin, R. A., Income and happiness, 2001, p.466; Oswald, A. J., Happiness and economic performance, 1997, p.1830.
[51] Cf. Ahuvia, A. C., Friedman, D. C., Income, Consumption, and Subjective Well-Being, 1998, p.155, 158, 161.
[52] Cf. Easterlin, R. A., Income and happiness, 2001, p.466; Oswald, A. J., Happiness and economic performance, 1997, p.1830.
[53] Cf. Ahuvia, A. C., Friedman, D. C., Income, Consumption, and Subjective Well-Being, 1998, p.155, 158, 161.

4. Closing

This last chapter will summarize the main findings of the assignment and provide a conclusion on the initial research question as well as a future outlook on the development of the topic analyzed.

4.1 Summary

Summarizing the main findings, the assignment has shown that economic growth and welfare have a strong impact on individuals' happiness and SWB which has proven to depend on material factors and economic prospects that raise individuals' living standards by increasing access to goods and services. Thus, the level of happiness can be measured to a certain extent by mayor economic determinants, which are particularly income, employment and inflation.

For all relationships between income and happiness, across countries, over time or between individuals within a country at a given point in time, income and happiness are in general positively related. However, happiness research has shown several reasons that the thesis of a higher income leading to a higher level of happiness due to an increasing access to goods and services is only partly true. First, income and happiness correlate in a curvilinear relationship, meaning a higher income provides increasing happiness at low levels of development but once a certain threshold has been passed, a further increase in income no longer contributes much to SWB. Second, an increase in income and the consumption of additional material goods and services only provide extra happiness temporarily and don't bear lasting effects on individuals' well-being due to the natural process of adaptation. Third, happiness is somehow relative and determined by continuous comparisons from individual's environment, their past or expectations of the future.

Regarding the relationship between employment and happiness, the assignment has outlined that regardless of whether unemployment is either seen as an unfortunate or voluntary state to be in, it reduces individual's level happiness in both cases. Happiness research has proven that unemployed persons are much less happy than employed ones - not solely due to a reduction of income but major psychological and social cost. However, the finding that employment increases happiness is not only due to the mere fact of having a job but particularly depending on other aspects as different types of work and occupations as well as individual's experienced work satisfaction.

Concerning the role of inflation on individuals' happiness, the effect does not depend on the distinction between predicted and unpredicted inflation and the possibility of adjustment or compensation. In contrast to the notion held in theoretical economics, the insights gained from happiness research suggest that inflation has a substantial negative effect on individuals' happiness quite irrespective of whether it is predicted or not. Either way, it causes a reduction of happiness as it introduces uncertainty about the future course of the economy. Individuals particularly fear a decrease in their purchasing power and thus also their standard of living.

4.2 Conclusion

Coming to a conclusion, the assignment has provided the answer to the introductory question as if economic growth and welfare affect individual's happiness and to what extent economic indicators such as income, employment and inflation are able to measure and contribute to individual's level of happiness and SWB.

On the one hand, the results and insights gained from the current state of happiness research presented in this assignment have shown that economic growth and welfare strongly affect individual's happiness and outlined the particular welfare effects of the major economic determinants income, employment and inflation on SWB.[54]

On the other hand, the presented insights have to be seen critically - not only regarding the mentioned limitations of the research methods and measurement results but also concerning the scope of analysis. The paradox and odd findings presented indicate that the economic is only one possible perspective to analyze the elusive concept of happiness. Although the major economic determinants presented are characterized as being in mutual relationship with other dependent variables that again have an effect on individual's happiness, there are still other important non-economic

---

[54] Cf. Frey, B., Stutzer, A., Happiness and Economics, 2002, p.171.

determinants independent from monetary or material goods that contribute to the level of SWB as well.[55]

Thus, the statement that money does not buy happiness has proven to be at least partly incorrect, but rather money can buy happiness only to a certain extent and only temporarily.

4.3 Future Outlook

Giving a future outlook on this topic, the systematic study of happiness in economics is only beginning and still in its initial stages. It is not surprising therefore, that the research undertaken so far leaves many questions open and important issues remain unresolved. At the same time, the insights gained from happiness research throw new light on important issues analyzed in economics and open up challenging new areas that have great potential to inspire future economic research. Further progress and improvements on happiness in economics are particularly expected in the following areas: application of more advanced estimation approaches in cross-national research and improved measurement methods that are applied to happiness research and economics. However, the success will be determined by and depending on the extent to which the new insights gained are integrated into established economics.[56]

---

[55] Cf. Ahuvia, A. C., Friedman, D. C., Income, Consumption, and Subjective Well-Being, 1998, p.154.
[56] Cf. Frey, B. S., Stutzer, A., Testing Theories of Happiness, 2005, p.116-146; Frey, B., Stutzer, A., Happiness and Economics, 2002, p.171-181; Frey, B. S., Stutzer, A., What Can Economists Learn from Happiness Research?, 2002, p.430f.

Bibliography

Frey, Bruno S., Stutzer, Alois (Recent Developments in the Economics of Happiness, 2013): Recent Developments in the Economics of Happiness, Cheltenham/Northhampton: Edward Elgar Publishing Limited, 2013

Frey, Bruno S., Stutzer, Alois (Testing Theories of Happiness, 2005): Testing Theories of Happiness, in: Bruni, Luigino, Porta, Pier L. (eds.), Economics and Happiness: Framing the Analysis, Oxford: Oxford University Press, 2005, p.116-146

Frey, Bruno S., Stutzer, Alois (Happiness and Economics, 2002): Happiness and Economics – How the Economy and Institutions affect Human Well-Being, New Jersey: Princeton University Press, 2002

Haucap, Justus, Heimeshoff, Ulrich (The Happiness of Economists, 2014): The Happiness of Economists: Estimating the Causal Effect on Studying Economics on Subjective Well-Being, Düsseldorf: dup, 2014

Heilbroner, Robert L., Milberg, William (The Making of Economic Society, 2011): The Making of Economic Society, 13th edition, New Jersey: Pearson Education, 2011

Helliwell, John, Layard, Richard, Sachs, Jeffrey (Eds.) (World Happiness Report, 2016): World Happiness Report 2016 Update, Vol.1, New York: SDSN, 2016

Jahan, Selim (Human Development Report, 2015): Human Development Report – Work for Human Development, New York: UNDP, 2015

Lis, Johannes (Nutzen oder Glück, 2014): Nutzen oder Glück: Möglichkeiten und Grenzen einer deontologisch-theoretischen Fundierung der economics of happiness, Stuttgart: Lucius & Lucius, 2014

Lucas, Richard E., Clark, Andrew E., Georgellis, Yannis, Diener, Ed (Unemployment, 2002): Unemployment Alters the Set-Point for Life Satisfaction, Paris: Delta, 2002

Mankiw, N. Gregory, Taylor, Mark P. (Grundzüge der Volkswirtschaftslehre, 2016): Grundzüge der Volkswirtschaftslehre, 6th edition, Stuttgart: Schäffer-Poeschel, 2016

Mankiw, N. Gregory, Taylor, Mark P. (Economics, 2014): Economics, 3rd edition, Hampshire: Cengage Learning EMEA, 2014

Peil, Jan, van Staveren, Irene (Handbook of Economics and Ethics, 2009): Handbook of Economics and Ethics, Nijmegen: Radboud University, 2009

Samuelson, Paul A., Nordhaus, William D. (Economics, 2010): Economics, 19th edition, New Delhi: Tata McGraw-Hill, 2010

Selin, Helaine, Davey, Gareth (Happiness Across Cultures, 2012): Happiness Across Cultures: Views of Happiness and Quality of Life in Non-Western Cultures, New York: Springer, 2012

Wessels, Walter J. (Economics, 2012): Economics, 4th edition, New York: Barron's Educational Series, 2012

Ahuvia, Aaron C., Friedman, Douglas C. (Income, Consumption, and Subjective Well-Being, 1998): Income, Consumption, and Subjective Well-Being: Toward a Composite Macromarketing Model, in: Journal of Macromarketing, Vol.18, p.153-168

Clark, Andrew E., Frijters, Paul, Shields, Michael A. (Relative Income, Happiness, and Utility, 2008): Relative Income, Happiness, and Utility: An Explanation for the Easterlin Paradox and Other Puzzles, in: Journal of Economic Literature, Vol.46, p.95-144

Cornelißen, Thomas (The interaction of Job Satisfaction, Job Search, and Job Changes, 2009): The interaction of Job Satisfaction, Job Search, and Job Changes. An Empirical Investigation with German Panel Data, in: Journal of Happiness Studies, Vol.10, p.367-384

Diener, Ed, Suh, Eunkook M., Lucas, Richard E., Smith, Heidi L. (Subjective Well-Being, 1999): Subjective Well-Being: Three Decades of Progress, in: Psychological Bulletin, Vol.125, p.276-302

Di Tella, Rafael, MacCulloch, Robert J., Oswald, Andrew J. (Preferences over Inflation and Unemployment, 2001): Preferences over Inflation and Unemployment: Evidence from Surveys of Happiness, in: The American Economic Review, Vol.91, p.335-341

Dixon, Huw D. (Controversy, 1997): Controversy: Economics and Happiness, in: The Economic Journal, Vol.107, p.1812-1814

Easterlin, Richard A. (Income and happiness, 2001): Income and happiness: towards a unified theory, in: The Economic Journal, Vol.111, p.465-484

Frey, Bruno S., Stutzer, Alois (What Can Economists Learn from Happiness Research?, 2002): What Can Economists Learn from Happiness Research?, in: Journal of Economic Literature, Vol.XL, p.402-435

Frey, Bruno S., Stutzer, Alois (Happiness, Economy and Institutions, 2000): Happiness, Economy and Institutions, in: The Economic Journal, Vol.110, p.918-938

Helliwell, John F., Huang, Haifang (Well-Being and Trust in the Workplace, 2011): Well-Being and Trust in the Workplace, in: Journal of Happiness Studies, Vol.12, p.747-767

Oswald, Andrew J. (Happiness and economic performance, 1997): Happiness and economic performance, in: The Economic Journal, Vol.107, p.1815-1831

Stevenson, Betsey, Wolfers, Justin (Economic Growth and Subjective Well-Being, 2008): Economic Growth and Subjective Well-Being: Reassessing the Easterlin Paradox, in: Brookings Papers on Economic Activity, Vol.39, p.1-87

Stutzer, Alois (The role of income aspirations in individual happiness, 2004): The role of income aspirations in happiness, in: Journal of Economic Behavior & Organization, Vol.54, p.89-109

Van Praag, Bernard M. S., Baarsma, Barbara E. (Using happiness surveys to value intangibles, 2005): Using happiness surveys to value intangibles: The case of airport noise, in. The Economic Journal, Vol. 115, p.224-246

Veenhoven, Ruut (Is happiness relative?, 1991): Is happiness relative?, in: Social Indicators Research, Vol.24, p.1-34

ITM-Checklist

Topics	The sine qua non of success	Comments/Suggestions
Economics	Which macroeconomic relevance is inherent in the topics?	In the economics area, checks must be undertaken to determine if and how the level of happiness may have an influence on individual behavior and important economic decisions like consumption activities.
Marketing	Which advantages and disadvantages arise out of the suggestions for marketing measures, external impact, and the company's general productivity? Which measures should be taken concerning internal and/or external marketing?	In the area of marketing, happiness research should be considered to understand consumer needs and behavior for developing a successful marketing strategy and corresponding activities in order to create the feeling of happiness in conjunction with the consumption of the products and services offered.
Human Resource Management	Which personnel consequences (quantitative or qualitative) result from the suggestions?	With regard to human resources, it is necessary to consider the role and importance of employees' happiness in the workplace and set up appropriate actions,

		e.g. reward and recognition programs.
Corporate Finance	What criteria have to be considered when choosing appropriate terms of financing? Which risks are existing and what kind of coverage is suggested? How should the influence of external factors be evaluated?	Corporate finance particularly deals with the monetary sense of happiness. Among other things, the analysis of financial performance is involved which has a strong influence on all share and stakeholders' happiness.
Strategic Corporate Management	How is the topic's strategic relevance to be evaluated, especially concerning the aspects of securing existence, competitive advantages, tying up resources, sustainability, and risks?	Strategic management involves including organizational goals as employee engagement and customer loyalty in the corporate strategy to improve the "Return on Happiness" and create a competitive advantage.
Business Law	Which legal fields are affected by the suggestions? What has to be arranged in order to create legal security from the company's point of view?	In the area of business law, the insights gained from happiness research should be considered for policy-making purpose within the organization.

Soft Skills & Leadership Qualities	Which demands does the realization of the suggestions require of the responsible managers? What leadership behavior is expedient?	Regarding soft skills and leadership qualities, it is important to consider the insights gained from happiness on the influence of employment and particularly work satisfaction on individuals' happiness. Happiness plays an integral role in this area as it supports good leadership qualities and in turn, good leadership qualities in terms of social skills and management styles can possibly also affect follower's level of happiness, e.g. through inspiration and motivation.
Research Methods	What sources of information should be practiced in order to stay up to date in the field of topics?	In the research methods area, employee and customer surveys should be undertaken regularly in form of interviews or questionnaires for happiness measures and analyses.
Management Decision Making	Which decision criteria should be practiced on the choice of alternatives?	In management decision-making, it is important to consider the psychological aspect of happiness. Emotions, and thus the level of happiness, have a strong influence

		on decision-processing in managerial decision-making situations.
Business Ethics and Sustainability	What relevant ethical question may arise in the given context? Which management measures could be useful to address these potential challenges effectively and efficiently? Which sustainability challenges may occur in the given context?	In business ethics, happiness should be considered the ultimate value proposition to establish ethical standards within the business environment and thus cultivate customer satisfaction and employee well-being. When dealing with sustainability, the company has to cope with the ecological and social responsibility. In this context, the development of a common philosophy for environmental and cultural consciousness may contribute positively to the collective level of happiness.